# Effective Techniques for Unarmed Combat

# Effective Techniques for Unarmed Combat

A contemporary self-defense system
scientifically developed from proven applications
of fighting techniques and principles

Mizhou Hui, M.D., Ph.D.

Multi-Media Books
Burbank, California

# Disclaimer

First published in 1999 by Multi-Media Books, an imprint of Unique Publications, Inc.

LCCN:
ISBN: 1-892515-20-2

Distributed by:
Unique Publications
4201 Vanowen Place
Burbank, CA 91505
(800) 332–3330

First edition
05 04 03 02 01 00 99 98 97 1 3 5 7 9 10 8 6 4 2

Printed in the United States of America

Interior and Cover Design by Dino Flores
Edited by Mark V. Wiley and Christopher D. Hess

# Table of Contents

# Introduction

The earliest origins of martial art practice in ancient China occurred in 208 B.C. Testimony to this was found in 1975 as a combative encounter carved in a wooden screen *(muli)* was found in an ancient tomb of Chinese Qin dynasty. This picture describes a combative competition performed on a stage, and was not unlike an ancient counterpart of today's Ultimate Fighting Championship. (Note that a referee is on the left in the drawing while two men are fighting on the right, and that they are all wearing distinguished belts.) Late in the 9th century, a written record titled *Jiaoliji* (Story of Wrestle and Fight), described details about this combative art known as jiaodi—which, translated, means to wrestle and fight.

Jiaodi was used to train soldiers for close quarter combat during the ancient state wars, and is the foundation upon which the various Chinese combative systems were built. It was the original form of modern day *san shou* (a Chinese national sport) and *daleitai* (a Chinese traditional combat competition on a stage). After the wars ended, these combat skills were incorporated into artistic and sport forms so that warriors could continue refining their skills and strengthening their bodies without the possibility of killing one another during training. These artistic forms were further developed and specialized into Chinese kickboxing (kung-fu), arm-locking (chin na), and wrestling (shuaijio).

Classical Chinese kung-fu systems were the next development in martial art practice in the East. It is believed that these classical systems were introduced into Japan in 1638 by a Min dynasty army general named Chen, who was sent to Japan to ask for reinforcement against the Medarian invasion into mainland China. It is believed that modern Oriental martial arts, including karate, judo, and taekwon-do, were developed based on modification of these Chinese classical systems by independent Japanese and Korean groups, while Western boxing and free-style wrestling were concurrently developed in the West.

Some of the most popular martial arts around the world today include karate, kung-fu, judo, free-style wrestling, and taekwondo. Sport boxing has also been a dominant martial art in the West for more than a century. After World War II, Japanese martial arts and culture spread rapidly and permeated the West. Some of these post-war expansions of Oriental martial arts include karate (a Japanese version of Chinese kung-fu) and judo (a Japanese version of Chinese wrestling and joint-locking). In addition, following the Korean war taekwondo penetrated into North America.

Some estimates suggest that these martial arts are practiced by perhaps as many as four million people, chiefly as competition sports. Of course, there are regulations and rules for competition to ensure the safety of the competitors. While this is good for martial sports, these regulations and rules suggest that those types of martial arts can not be considered realistic for unarmed combat or self-defense.

Despite the proliferation of martial art as sport, I have observed an increasing trend among many martial artists to pursue the original combat form of martial art for self-defense. For those ready to embrace that pursuit, this manual provides the skills necessary to meet the challenge.

As a medical doctor, research scientist, and a martial artist with thirty years of training and teaching experience, I have identified the two most important elements that govern the effectiveness of combat martial art—momentum and leverage. These two elements are the most commonly employed in all effective unarmed combat and self-defense techniques. Understanding these two elements will greatly enhance your training and the effectiveness of your skills.

Momentum and leverage with mechanical disadvantage for generation of boxing speed will be described in Seminar One, "The Principle of Power in Punches and Strikes," and Seminar Two, "Guiding Principles for Kickboxing." Specifically, the use of leverage with mechanical advantage for arm-locks will be addressed in Seminar Three, "Three Universal Principles Governing Effective Arm-Lock Skills."

In this book, important principles including body mechanics, human anatomy, and military tactics of war arts are used to improve the effectiveness of unarmed combat and self-defense skills. These principles will also be applied to kickboxing skills and its training. Normal, everyday language is used instead of professional biomechanical and medical terms so that they can be easily understood.

This book is designed to be a standard reference book for martial arts instructors and a teaching manual for police officers and army soldiers. It is also designed as a self-learning manual for those who desire to learn unarmed self-defense. By summarizing my life-long practice and teaching experience in martial arts and using my scientific training background, the most relevant principles governing effective unarmed combat and self-defense are presented here for anyone willing to study and learn.

I have also summarized the most effective "smart fighting" skills in this book. These skills have been objectively tested for many years—both in the East and West—and are based on realistic situations such as when a physically weaker person is confronted with a physically stronger person. Smart fighting means employing skills based on sound, scientific principles such as applied biomechanics.

Although biomechanical research has been used to improve non-martial art sports training for many decades, many question whether they are relevant in improving the effectiveness of martial art training and techniques. Whether consciously or not, however, all martial artists have made use of these scientific principles in their techniques. This explains why their "no nonsense" techniques have been widely accepted by different cultures and effectively passed from generation to generation. This book, therefore, is an attempt to start the process of understanding what these principles are and their application in analyzing our techniques and improving our training.

# A PRIMER

## Biomechanical Principles of Levers

Before proceeding to the seminars, a review of the "two-lever system," which governs the effectiveness of martial art skills, is presented below. In terms of a two-lever system, a muscular bone lever with mechanical advantage will be used for arm-locking and wrestling, while a muscular bone lever with mechanical disadvantage will be used for generation of striking speed and power in kickboxing. The leverage with mechanical advantage and disadvantage are illustrated below for better visualization and understanding.

Careful consideration of these principles and the benefits they offer illustrate the types of advantages available to readers who employ the principles outlined in the seminars that follow.

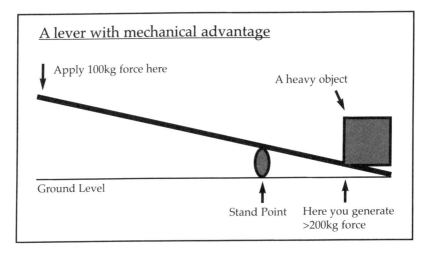

A lever with mechanical advantage

Apply 100kg force here

A heavy object

Ground Level

Stand Point    Here you generate
>200kg force

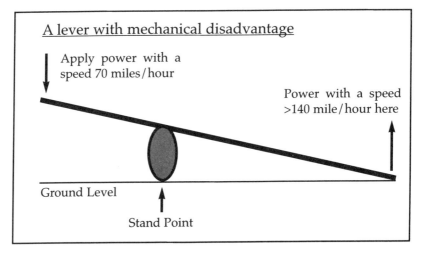

A lever with mechanical disadvantage

Apply power with a speed 70 miles/hour

Power with a speed >140 mile/hour here

Ground Level

Stand Point

# SEMINAR 1

## The Principle of Power
## in Punches and Strikes

In unarmed combat, punching power is the result of applying one's muscle force to accelerate one's fist strike optimally together with one's body weight. If a technique has tremendous force but inadequate speed (velocity), it is not powerful. Conversely, if a technique has tremendous speed but inadequate force, it becomes nothing more than a tap on the shoulder. Therefore, in this seminar I emphasizes both force and speed in the delivery of truly powerful techniques.

Understanding the biomechanical principles that govern human movement is very helpful. For instance, striking power is best referred to as momentum, and is the result of applying one's muscle force. A fast moving object contains striking power since momentum equals mass (weight) times velocity (speed with specific direction). Striking power can also be understood in the context of a collision of a fast moving truck into a wall. The higher the speed of the truck, the more damage it causes. Furthermore, the truck causes more damage when it is heavily loaded. This is why true power is weight (mass) times speed (velocity). This explains why, besides speed, body weight matters in boxing and wrestling.

Many martial artists wonder how to deliver a punch with the greatest impact. Does maximal impact occur when striking the opponent from the side? Head-on? The impact on the target from a linear striking power can be defined as the change in momentum divided by the time it takes to change.

Complete release of the striking power on the target results from complete deceleration of a fast moving object by the target. Therefore, to achieve the most impact, throw a linear strike to your opponent when he is charging or committed to charging toward you. This will generate the maximum impact on the target.

To further achieve the optimal momentum or striking power, one should throw (not push) their hand toward an intended target (with maximum speed), and move their

Fig. 3

body weight simultaneously with it to create a large mass. This is power: weight times speed. Power can be further enhanced by the landing or "shaking down" of the body together with the impact of your hand on the target (Figure 3).

As an example, Bruce Lee's powerful "three inch punch" was generated in part by a kind of "body shaking" motion. Here, two principles must be reiterated and emphasized. First, the speed of the hand at the instant of contact is crucial for power. Second, at the instant of contact, tensing the arm and shoulder muscles simultaneously allows body weight to be used as an effective mass to enhance punches or strikes.

The effective mass associated with powerful momentum also originates in the proper alignment of the forearm, upper arm, and shoulder. Hitting straight-on allows the momentum of the upper body and arms to be transferred to the hand.

You could charge a person more powerfully with the help of an assisted run. Thus, you can enhance your striking speed by initiating your attack with the help of a sudden stepping on the ground (Figure 3a). Sport science researchers have noted that Mike Tyson's powerful strikes are related to the stepping power of his strong legs.

Based on the principles outlined thus far, it should be clear that a truly powerful punch can not be completed by a single arm motion. It must be a coordinated whole body motion. Further, human hands and feet are connected to the body by two joints. Therefore, other than speed and use of body weight, friction or resistance force from the joints associated with their tightened ligaments, tendons, or generated from contracting muscles toward different directions may also affect striking power by reducing the speed of a coordinated whole-body motion.

Fig. 3a

As a practical example, initiating a jab by relaxing the shoulder, elbow, and wrist reduces the joint, ligament, and muscle tendon resistance, thus indirectly increasing your striking speed. This is often observed during professional boxing. Therefore, avoiding the generation of unwanted resistance by internal muscle tightening should be emphasized.

The backward motion of the right shoulder can also be used while initiating a left jab to achieve additional power (Figure 4). In scientific terms, it is the transfer of a centrical force into a linear striking power. It has double effects: increasing one's striking speed and security (one's face is moving away from a possible counter jab).

Fig. 4

It would be ideal to use all the above-mentioned power sources to achieve an optimal strike (which is illustrated in Figs. 5a, b, showing a typical step-in jab in boxing). However, this can be difficult in reality. In professional boxing, for instance, a fighter who knows how to deliver truly powerful punches featuring force, speed, body shaking, and a straight-on linear impact may wait through multiple rounds before delivering a knock-out punch.

In other types of unarmed combat besides boxing, opponents, while in constant motion, must be ready to initiate a strike at any time. Persistent practice of the principles that govern powerful punches and strikes can prepare anyone for these situations. Here are a few more principles that should also be practiced.

Fig. 5a                    Fig. 5b

For a rear hand linear strike, body rotation is the most important source of power. Combative athletes often wonder how one can rotate quickly enough to reach an opponent without being countered during the rotation. In biomechanical science, the shorter the rotation radius, the faster the rotation will. This is illustrated by a figure skater's spin (rotation of the body) on ice. The fastest body rotation can only be achieved by landing one foot (blade) on the ice and holding the arms close to the body.

Scientifically, this can be interpreted by the shortened radius of rotation and the reduced area for friction on ice. In boxing, fast body rotation for a linear strike from the rear (right) hand can be achieved by planting the front foot on the ground and shifting the body weight on it as quickly as possible and then rotating the body (Figures 6a–c, top and back views). During rotation, lean the body to the left (Figure 6b, top and back view). This will cause a shift of the body's longitudinal axis away from the rotation axis and speed up the rotation by making it more balanced and reduce the relative radius of rotation. The same holds true for a centrifugation motion: without balanced weight, it simply will not spin.

Angular strikes, such as hooks or hook-like punches, are dominant means of achieving knock-outs in professional boxing. The power of angular strikes is governed by angular momentum, which is defined as body weight times the squared radius of gyration times angular velocity. Therefore, power training for hooks is a matter of how to generate angular momentum.

For hooks, the radius of gyration is the distance between the body center and the striking fist. This distance is extremely important for issuing striking power since it is proportional to the square of the radius of gyration. In fact, this is making use of a leverage with mechanical disadvantage in order to obtain speed and then momentum. In other words, you have a short but strong muscular bone lever arm to apply force in order to achieve high speed at the far end of the long lever arm. This can be

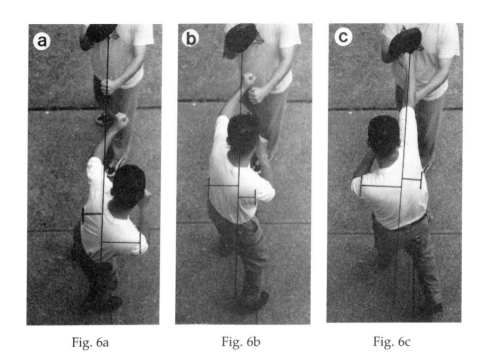

Fig. 6a          Fig. 6b          Fig. 6c

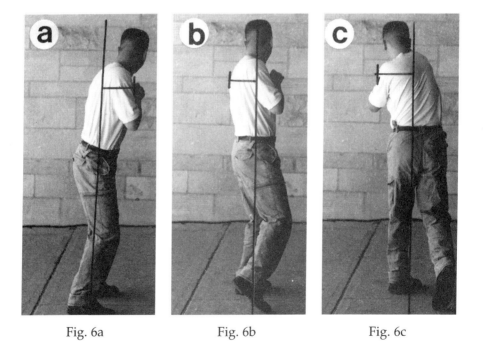

Fig. 6a          Fig. 6b          Fig. 6c

demonstrated by the fact that a longer stick can hit a target much harder than a shorter one. This also explains why boxers are unable to deliver powerful hooks when their bodies are too close to one another. Initiating a hook at the moment of separation between the two bodies is therefore recommended for optimal power.

It is important to initiate hooks with body rotation rather than an arm motion since body rotation is the most important power source for hooks. Aside from the body rotation, the head and upper trunk should move in the opposite direction from an attack. Figure 7 shows that the trunk goes to the left of the opponent while the opponent's head is hooked from the right. This head and upper trunk motion hides the attack from the opponent while directly increasing the hook's power.

Fig. 7

The fist is connected to the lower arm with two joints. Interestingly, this particular anatomy structure enables human beings to be better at throwing a strike with an angular path than with a linear one. This is partially because of power resistance from the joint, tendon, and ligament friction of the system against the angular motion. Therefore, completely straight punches do not work as efficiently or economically as do slightly angular ones. Moreover, the path, angle, and timing of the circular strike is more difficult for an opponent to predict than a straight strike, so this is a tactical advantage as well.

The principles outlined in this first seminar enable any reader to understand the biomechanical principles governing powerful punches and strikes. Moreover, these principles are useful for analyzing your current techniques and improving your training methods, regardless of your present style or rank.

# SEMINAR 2

## Guiding Principles
## for Kickboxing

Kickboxing is an extremely complex sport. It is not only governed by biomechanical principles, human anatomy, and physiology but also involves human intelligence (combat tactics) and human fitness (strength and conditioning). This complexity is the primary reason that no complete, comprehensive scientific theory has yet been developed for kickboxing training.

However, in this seminar, certain body mechanics, human anatomy, and military tactics of war arts are addressed to improve the effectiveness of kickboxing skills and their training. As noted previously, easy to understand, everyday language, is used instead of highly technical, professional, biomechanical, and medical terms so that any reader can more easily understand and thus apply these principles.

As discussed in Seminar 1, striking power is a matter of how to generate maximum momentum in the shortest period of time by applying muscle force. Hard and correct training helps condition one's muscle more efficiently. Initiation speed is vitally important to deliver the most effective, lethal strikes. However, there is a limit for our human race and sometimes we just are able to move faster than others. Therefore, during unarmed combat in or out of the ring, achieving momentum without being detected by an opponent is perhaps the most important component of success. Thus, a feint move or natural move (which is not recognized by your opponent as a preparation for an attack) is needed to set-up a technique with substantial momentum. This is the foundation for a combination attack, since in a combination a previous move is always required to prepare a secondary move for a powerful strike.

There are four important principles involved in effective kickboxing to establish a powerful technique without being detected. Before these principles are listed with applications for kickboxing combat, however, please be aware of the most important consideration: personal safety. This is the first priority. Always remember that you may be countered whenever a technique is initiated. Therefore, all techniques must be considered within the context of this personal safety consideration: that any attack may mean a response of equal or greater threat to personal safety. So, choose your techniques wisely!

Now we're ready for the four guiding principles for kickboxing. By employing all of these principles in training and competition, effective techniques capable of prevailing over an opponent are possible.

---

**•PRINCIPLE 1:**

Prepare a powerful strike without being noticed

**•PRINCIPLE 2:**

Understand timing and how to use distance

**•PRINCIPLE 3:**

Use safe angled passes to close in for a counter strike

**•PRINCIPLE 4:**

Use proper blocking to close in for a counter strike

---

In the following paragraphs, several examples are employed to demonstrate how the personal safety rule and these guiding principles are applied to kickboxing techniques. First, however, let's review the definition of "angulation." Angulation describes a safe angled pass to close the gap between you and your opponent. In figure 8a, the linear distance (from top view) between your eyes and your opponent's eyes at the moment before your opponent is committed to his motion for an attack is defined as a base line (zero degree). To avoid a linear punch at zero degree, your head must move together with your trunk away from the line of attack. Meanwhile, the gap between yourself and your opponent must be close to allow for a counter-attack (figure 8b). This coordinated motion is called angulation or safe angled pass to close in. This angulation motion is used to close-the-gap safely and always goes together with proper blocking and counter-action.

To utilize the first principle of preparing a powerful strike without being noticed, try catching your opponent after he has committed to an attack. For example, in figure 8a and b, the demonstrator counter-attacks his opponent with a jab when the opponent is committed to his jab attack. In this way, the person in black is unable to escape from the counter-attack because of his commitment to the attack. In other words, by his commitment to a particular technique, you have the perfect opportunity to deliver your own technique without being noticed.

The complete deceleration of a moving object generates the maximum power according to the definition of striking power. This is because the two meeting forces (i.e., your jab meeting his forward moving face) are larger than one force. Safe angled passes or angulation (an arrow indicates trunk motion toward the left) and proper blocking are also employed with the timing in this example to safely close-the-gap when you step in to deliver a counter-attack (Figure 8b). This, therefore, incorporates principle three as well.

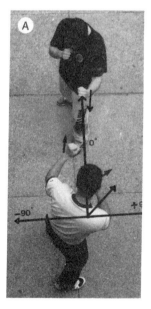

Fig. 8a               Fig. 8b

The second guiding principle is understanding timing and how to use distance. This principle is illustrated in figures 9a, b. In this example, the opponent (in the black shirt) is committed to a rear hand punch while the demonstrator (in the white shirt) simultaneously counters him with a front hand jab. Since the distance from a rear hand to the face is longer than from a jab to the face, the jab should land first. This counter move is effective because it makes good use of difference in distance and timing.

Fig. 9a                Fig. 9b

Another example of using timing, in combination with preparing powerful strikes without being noticed, is illustrated in figure 10. When you are attacked with a jab, your rear hand together with your front shoulder must block it on time (Figure 10a, b). At this point you should start to swing your front hand underneath your opponent's arms to set up momentum to strike the side of his head with both power and surprise (Figure 10c). Since this is an angular strike motion or whip-hook, the time of landing your fist on the target can be manipulated. For instance, delayed landing of your hook strike can sometimes confuse your opponent. Remember that one of Bruce Lee's famous fighting stances featured his rear hand posed higher (to guard his face) and his front hand lower (ready for a counter-attack).

The second guiding principle not only considers timing but also distance. Techniques that effectively use dis-

| Fig.10a | Fig. 10b | Fig. 10c |

tance are illustrated in figure 11. As noted previously, a feint move can be used to prepare a powerful strike. For example, a sweeping kick is a very powerful kick. However, it is easily detected and countered. Conducting a feinting rear punch, started at an unrealistic distance, with your body turned slightly to the left, prepares your body for the sweeping kick. A feinting rear punch also provides you with a safe distance and jamming effect that avoids your opponent's possible counter-jab. This move (figures 11a, b) sets up a powerful sweeping kick to the opponent's lower leg without being detected. It also causes your opponent to lose balance while incurring serious injury (figure 11c).

As noted, the combined use of several of these guiding principles in one technique characterizes an excellent technique. In terms of this feint with a sweeping kick,

Fig.11a              Fig. 11b                 Fig. 11c

the body rotation speed is vitally important. Speeding up the rotation for a sweeping kick requires quickly shifting your body weight on one foot and then rotating. Further, stepping, punching, and rotating should be done together as a coordinated whole body motion (Figure 11b).

The fourth important guiding principle employs the use of blocking. As many techniques employ a variety of principles (preferably all of them!), figure 12a-d demonstrates how the

Fig.12a

Fig.12b

combined use of feinting, timing, proper blocking, angulation, and use of an opponent's resistance prepares momentum without being detected.

To illustrate this point, an offensive "first strike" jab is used in anticipation of an opponent's possible jab, (figures 12a, b). Forward momentum is also used to close in with him (figures 12b, c). Further, the motion of the clashing forearms will allow use of his resistance to circle the lead arm around his lead arm (figures 12c, d).

Fig.12c

Fig.12d

During this circling, the opponent's lead arm is checked by the right rear hand for safety. This circling, rotating, and leaning of the body sets up the moving momentum for a powerful, whipping hook (figure 12d). The positioning of the head and torso serves as a distraction while preparing for a strike from the other side. Furthermore, these motions also provide a safe position against possible counter-strikes.

The lead arm is used both for blocking and counter-striking as it is the safest and most efficient weapon. Due to the proximity of the lead hand to the opponent, it is quicker to deliver a counter strike. The whipping motion is aimed at the blind side of the opponent, making it difficult for him to see the oncoming blow.

Fig. 13a

Fig. 13b

One final technique that, again, employs a variety of the guiding principles, and has been found to be very effective, is the use of feinting motions and centrical force to prepare a powerful back-kick. A feinting move (a jab started at a distance a little further than realistic) with a side-stepped and half-turned body (figure 13a, b) sets up a body rotation motion which generates a centrical force (figure 13c). This centrical force contains momentum which is released and transferred into a powerful back-kick aimed at the opponent (figure 13d)

Once the human brain is accelerated to a certain degree, loss of consciousness occurs. In turn, acceleration of the head is a measure of experiencing the "knock-out" in kickboxing, boxing, or in any other type of combat.

Fig. 13c

Fig. 13d

In one sense, brain acceleration leading to knock out is understood similar to the definition that deceleration of a momentum or a moving object by the target is a measure of the striking power. In other words, in order to accelerate the brain of a large opponent, more momentum is required.

Of particular interest to readers, an opponent with a strong and short neck will be more difficult to knock-out since his head is simply more stable. However, even with a short, strong neck, an opponent can be knocked out if he experiences sufficient force. This type of "sufficient force" occurs with large mass. That is why body weight plays a key role in delivering a knock-out punch.

Aside from the body weight of the attacker and strength of the opponent's neck, several other factors must be considered. Many readers may have noticed a knock-out in professional boxing frequently involves a hook punch to the jaw. This can be at least partially understood by human anatomy and human mechanics. By design, the human brain is well protected by strong skull bones, while the head is supported and fixed by groups of strong muscles originating from the skull and attached to the shoulders and trunk. It is very difficult to shake the human brain to the extent of injury.

However, the impact of a hook on the jaw is critical and can shake the brain through a joint axis (figure 14). This impact is proportionally amplified on the brain through a longer lever arm, from the jaw to the axis, which is much longer than that from the axis to the brain. This impact-affected change of head velocity or acceleration of the brain is mainly responsible for brain injuries among boxers. The change of velocity or brain acceleration will stretch or shear the brain tissue and cause damage. Humans lose consciousness when the acceleration reaches a certain level (a "knock-out"). Moreover, unawareness of an on-coming strike also plays a role in a knock-out experience.

Readers engaged in combat situations should concentrate on stabilizing their head and "shortening" their neck by

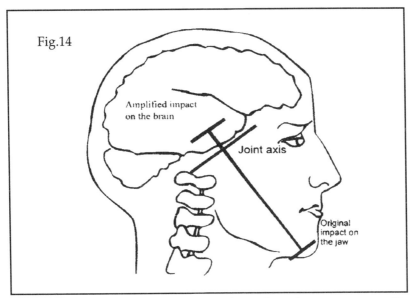

Fig.14

Amplified impact
on the brain

Joint axis

Original
impact on
the jaw

constricting the neck muscles when they become immediately aware of an on-coming strike. However, hooking strikes usually come from the side and are difficult to detect until it is too late.

The final factor involved in effective kickboxing, and combat in general, is psychological. Two Chinese military proverbs help illustrate the importance of psychology in unarmed combat. The first proverb states: "The brave shall win when two matched armies meet in a narrow valley." This suggests that if someone is fearless the chances of hesitation while initiating an attack are minimal—which will optimize speed and power. The second proverb states: "Deal with a changing situation by no change." In kickboxing, this can be interpreted as the use of well-trained skills or inborn superiority to cope with any variety of opponents with differing fighting styles. First apply well-trained skills instead of trying to discover an opponent's weakness. By the time a weakness is determined, it may be too late in combat reality.

Understanding the principles and discussion in Seminar 2 should enable readers to understand the scientific principles which govern the kickboxing techniques and training, and, more importantly, how to apply them to analyze techniques and improve training. Hopefully, all martial artists, regardless of their styles and origins, will agree that understanding the scientific principles that govern the effectiveness of human movements can make martial art training more efficient and more predictable.

# SEMINAR 3

## Principles Governing Effective
## Arm-Lock Skills

Arm-locking skills are important aspects of unarmed combat. The effectiveness of such skills can be witnessed in bouts—such as those found in the Ultimate Fighting Championships—where many victories are determined by the various joint locks and submission techniques. In addition to their competitive use, arm-locking skills are the distilled essence of simplicity, directness, and practicality. This is a primary reason why they are used so extensively in police unarmed combat training.

These arm-locking skills utilize three important universal principles when the techniques are successful. These principles include leverage, anatomical and physiological strengths of the body, and the philosophy of war. When these three principles are combined into an arm-lock technique, the result will be both efficient and effective.

**Use of Leverage**

Arm-locking employs the "lever" principle. In biomechanics, torque equals the length of the lever arm times force used. For instance, an illustration of torque can be observed while unscrewing a nut using a wrench. The longer the

Fig.17

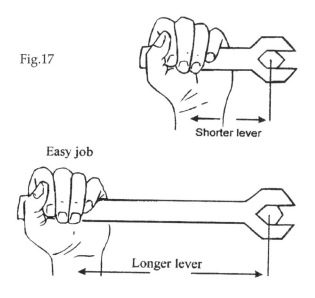

Shorter lever

Easy job

Longer lever

wrench (lever arm), the larger the force (torque) on the nut (Figure 17).

The leverage principle enables a quicker and effective arm-lock while offering the practitioner a measure of safety, as illustrated in Figures 18a-c.

In order to lock an opponent's grappling arm, extend his arm first by leaning back to obtain a longer lever and a larger torque (Figures 18a, b). Then, his wrist or elbow joint can be easily locked by employing body rotation (Figure 18c). Please note that in figure 18b, the subject is leaning back while initiating an arm-lock. This leaning back is both for safety (creating distance) and to use body gravity to extend

Fig.18a

Fig.18b

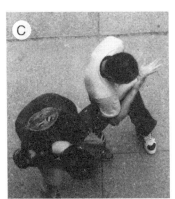

Fig.18c

the opponent's arm. In addition, this leaning back motion also makes body rotation easier and the joint-lock faster. It can be said that one technique employing various principles always characterizes an excellent martial art technique.

### Anatomical and Physiological Strengths

The knowledge of human anatomy and its physiological (or structural) strengths can enable anyone to disable an opponent with frightening efficiency. Furthermore, this knowledge will enable anyone to immobilize, incapacitate, and break joints, tendons, and ligaments with relative ease. Therefore, the knowledge and application of anatomical and structural strengths plays a vital role in effective combat and self-defense training.

Figures 19a-d demonstrate how the knowledge of human anatomy is employed to fend off an opponent who initiates a choking technique. In figure 19a, the victim is pushed against a wall and choked by an opponent. The first response should be to push the opponent's choking hands to the inside (figure 19b). Why push inside instead of directing the choking hands outward? Interestingly, the human body is constructed and trained to release more muscular force when pushing inside than opening out. This illustrates why it is important to understand anatomical and physiological strengths.

This pushing inside technique initially releases someone from the choking attack. Then, by using the momentum of this motion as shown in figure 19c, the opponent's right arm can be locked under both of the defender's arms (figure 19d). This final motion creates absolute superiority and disarms the opponent.

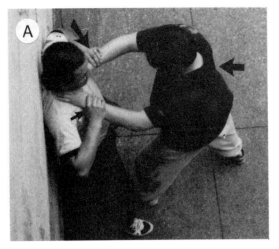

Fig.19a

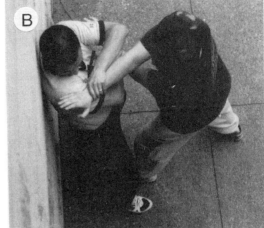

Fig.19b

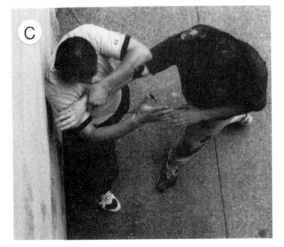

Fig.19c

Fig.19d

## The Philosophy of War

The Chinese military serves as an excellent example of using all three of the principles addressed in this seminar. In fact, the Chinese military trains and employs techniques that feature leverage, the knowledge of anatomical strengths, and, importantly, all physical techniques are further governed by ancient Chinese strategies and philosophies of war.

Rather than being outdated treatises on war and combat, the war classics serve as important references by providing guiding principles useful in modern warfare. Their complete understanding enables combatants to understand the nature of fighting situations, formulate proper strategies, and be better prepared in both armed and unarmed combat situations. For instance, "local superiority" is one of the Chinese military's primary principles. In martial application, this can be interpreted as defeating a stronger opponent by concentrating on his weak points, like the joints.

Figures 20a-c show how local superiority is created when both hands are grabbed by an opponent. When grabbed as shown in figure 20a, drop the left arm by using gravity and pulling it against your upper trunk. Next, catch the aggressor's grappling arm (specifically, the wrist) with your right hand (figure 20b). Then, rotate your body to your right in order to extend the opponent's arm and lock his wrist/elbow joints under your two arms against your trunk (figure 20c). In this technique, the lever principle and creation of local superiority are employed together to deliver an effective arm-lock.

Fig. 20a

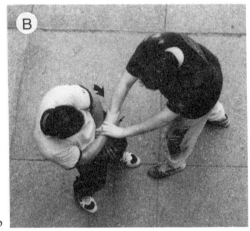

Fig. 20b

Fig. 20c

# SEMINAR 4

## Combat Wrestling Techniques

Combat wrestling features very complex techniques and is considered by some as the ultimate challenge of realistic martial arts. Arguably, it is the most dominant means for unarmed combat. This has been repeatedly demonstrated in unarmed combat competitions, such as the Ultimate Fighting Championships.

In the East, Chinese sport wrestling (shuaijiao) was the earliest form of wrestling, although Mongolians are the best known wrestler's of the region. Japanese judo, the best known jacket wrestling system in this century, is also a distinctive type of sport wrestling.

As a child growing up in Mongolia, I was fortunate to have gained extensive training experience in both jacket and non-jacket wrestling. Chinese country-style wrestling was very popular in my homeland. It does not require any form of wrestling jacket but applies similar rules of official Chinese sport wrestling. The major difference between country-style wrestling and official Chinese sport wrestling is the matter of wearing a wrestling jacket or not (a short sleeve version of the judo uniform). Technically speaking, the difference is whether or not you have easy access to grappling sites to apply power for a throw, in terms of jacket versus non-jacket wrestling.

In non-jacket wrestling, neck-holds, arm-holds, and leg-holds are the only available sites for applying powerful techniques.

Whether or not you have these sites available for holding determines which techniques should be employed.

In this seminar, I will introduce several practical skills which focus on defending against stronger opponents. Most of these skills are non-jacket dependent and are more realistic in terms of combat in the summer, although they can also be applied to an opponent with a wrestling jacket. However, in the cold or when engaged with a military-type opponent, heavy coats and military uniforms do serve as a kind of wrestling jacket.

To assist the reader's estimate of these techniques, figure 21 depicts the relative size of the demonstrators. From left to right are Igor G. Muskatblit, second degree black belt; author Matthew Hui; and Edmond Tsoi, first degree black belt.

Fig. 21

## The Neck-Hold Throw

This is the most commonly employed combat wrestling skill and has two versions. The size of the opponent will determine which version to use.

### Version One:

When dealing with a shorter opponent, you can easily close in with a counter charge and grab his neck and one of his arms as shown in Figure 22a. Next, pull the opponent toward you by loading your body weight on his neck, while turning your back forward (figure 22b), and then suddenly follow his resistance to close in (figures 22b, c). This motion is designed to make use of his resistance force by giving him feinting force and then suddenly following it to close-the-gap. After closing in, double lock your opponent's head and upper arm (figures 22c, d). At this point of the double lock, your victory is guaranteed.

Next, lean forward and turn your face to the other side, and then throw the opponent with a sudden pivoting motion as shown in figures 22d, e. In other words, pivoting is rotating with him. Turning your face to the other side will help your pivot. After he falls, do not lose your hold on his arm. Rather, insert your knee underneath his arm and then lock it between your knees as shown in figure 22f. Besides use of this arm-lock, you can also strike him or choke him in order to achieve complete ground control.

Fig. 22a

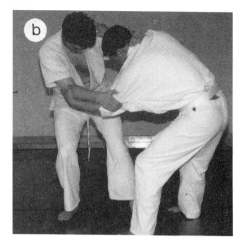

Fig. 22b

Fig. 22c

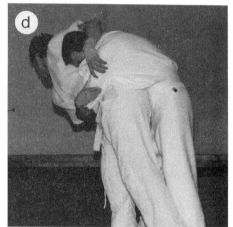

Fig. 22d

Fig. 22e

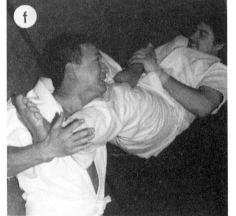

Fig. 22f

**Version Two:**

When dealing with a stronger opponent, the version one neck-hold throw by pivoting motion may not work well. Therefore, a modification is introduced. When you close in with your opponent by the similar motions described in version one, put him in a double-lock (head lock and upper arm lock) as shown in figures 23a, b. At this point, your opponent may move backward to resist your throw (figures 23b, c). Instead of throwing him forward with a

pivoting motion, release your lock at his arm and lock his neck with both of your hands as tight as possible (figure 23c). Once again, at this point your victory is guaranteed

Next, suddenly load all of your power on the opponent's isolated neck and crush him to the ground (figure 23c, d). This sudden force to his neck will most likely cause serious injury. For total domination, press his eye using your thumb to make him lose consciousness (figure 23d). When dealing with a taller and stronger opponent that cannot be thrown over by raw strength, this skill is the most realistic and effective technique of combat wrestling.

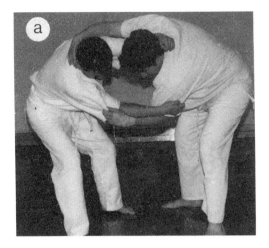

Fig. 23a

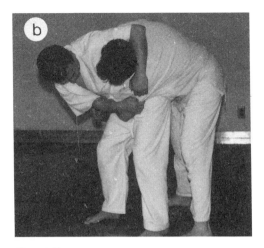

Fig. 23b

Fig. 23c

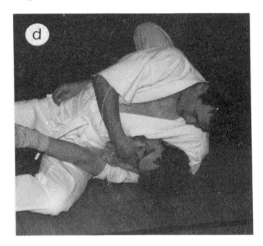

Fig. 23d

## Defense Against Leg-Hold

As depicted in figure 24a, an opponent may grab one of your legs. Clearly, you are now in an unfavorable situation. The following technique can enable anyone to overcome this situation.

Your first reaction is to insert your leg into his groin area and balance yourself by hooking either of his legs against his immediate throwing efforts (figure 24a). Once you have stabilized yourself, grab his waist belt and suddenly withdraw your inserted leg as shown in figure 24b. Then, throw the opponent by kicking and blocking his left shin with your withdrawn foot and suddenly throw him forward to the ground with a whole-body motion (figures 24c, d). You can also crush the opponent on the ground by falling on top of him. Then, striking, choking, eye-pressing, or using an arm-lock can be easily followed to finish-off the opponent.

Fig. 24a

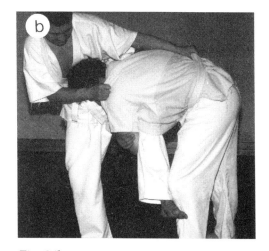

Fig. 24b

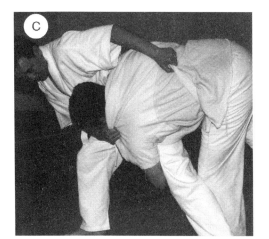

Fig. 24c

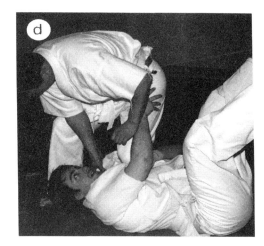

Fig. 24d

## Hook and Throw

When dealing with an opponent in a grappling situation as depicted in figure 25a, pull the opponent toward you by loading on your body weight. This will cause him to instinctively resist your pulling force. Once you feel his resistance, suddenly follow it by pushing him backwards while hooking one of his legs from outside to throw him (figures 25b-d). This technique is a typical application of the combat philosophy of "borrowing your opponent's force." Another method to set up this technique is kneeing or kicking the opponent's groin and then hooking the inside leg while the opponent is neutralized.

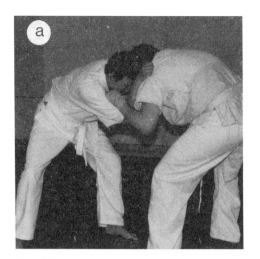

Fig. 25a

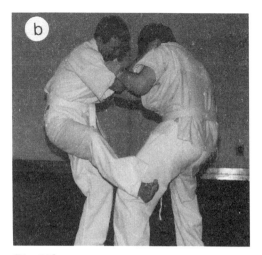

Fig. 25b

Fig. 25c

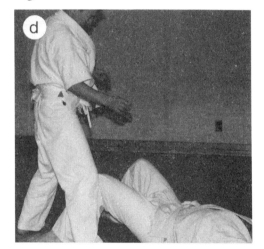

Fig. 25d

This throw will hurt the opponent considerably on both his back and head so he will probably not be able to react to your secondary move to close in and finish him off on the ground. Once the opponent is on the ground, strikes or choking techniques can be employed as depicted in figures 26a–f.

Readers will notice that combat wrestling is very different from any form of sport wrestling. Success requires the use of several important principles.

To understand the combat aspect of wrestling, you must first understand how to close in safely on your opponent without being counter-punched or kicked. Proper blocking and use of safe angles are primary strategies. However, the most important principle is to use correct timing.

As an example, try closing in with a counter charge whenever your opponent is committed to his forward move for an attack so that he will not be able to escape from your closing-in maneuver. This strategy is extremely effective when dealing with a fast kickboxer. Otherwise, you will never catch him. Clearly, a successful closing-in maneuver requires superior timing since the outcome of the technique can literally be determined in hundredths of a second.

Besides the closing-in technique, find grappling sites to apply power for throws. Without a jacket, grappling sites are limited to the neck, arms, legs and waist belt. This is the major reason that most of jacket wrestling techniques do not work well in unarmed combat.

Pivoting or body-rotation power is required to throw or unbalance your opponent. Pivoting power is conducted by pivoting yourself with your opponent to offset him. Pivoting actually makes use of leverage. Besides pivoting, explosive power is required for a successful throw, which requires an emphasis on force and speed.

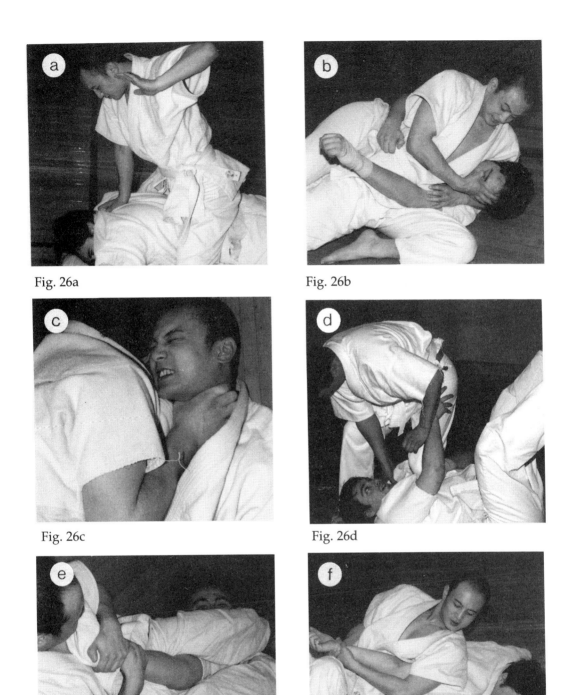

Fig. 26a

Fig. 26b

Fig. 26c

Fig. 26d

Fig. 26e

Fig. 26f

Besides explosive power, coordinated whole-body motion effectively uses one's body weight to enhance power. Numerous combat athletes refer to "borrowing an opponent's power" or "following his force" to offset him. You can easily follow an opponent's resistance force to throw him by first applying a feint and thereby causing him to resist.

It is important to remember that merely throwing an opponent may or may not finish him off. It partially depends on the surface nature of the ground and nearby objects. Therefore, follow through with a throw by striking, choking, strangling, eye-pressing, or arm-locking. Once again, figures 26a-f show the ideal positions to defeat an opponent on the ground in combat wrestling.

The positions depicted in figures 26af are the ideal positions for combat wrestling. Achieving a neck-hold is perhaps the most ideal position since the head-lock, strangling from behind, and eye-press are then convenient methods for a lethal attack. Also remember that creating local superiority by attacking lethal areas is a key when facing a stronger opponent.

# SEMINAR 5

## Unarmed Knife
## Defense Techniques

Unarmed self-defense against a knife-wielding assailant is a serious topic. It is a matter of life and death! Fancy, or showy knife defense techniques are inappropriate when life or limbs are on the line. The main goal of such an encounter is survival! The skills introduced in this seminar are highly distinguishable from unrealistic or fancy knife defense skills.

Simplicity and effectiveness are fundamental features of good unarmed knife defense skills. In reality, there is often no time to plan a defense when attacked by a knife-wielding opponent. Sophisticated techniques will simply be too difficult to execute in such chaotic situations.

People therefore wonder how to defend themselves from a knife attack. Running away is arguably the best policy when dealing with almost any kind of knife attack. Running away is strategic in that potential assistance can be obtained (e.g., police) or, perhaps, superior weapons can be obtained. Running away or attempting to run away can also provide an unique opportunity to trap a knife attacker so as to defeat him.

When dealing with a knife threat, an experienced martial artist may not have a problem in handling an inexperienced knife holder with arm-lock techniques. However, it is difficult to deal with a knife attack by blocking, catching, and arm-locking. These kinds of techniques are better used with a weaker or inexperienced attacker. But, since it is difficult to know whether an assailant is inexperienced, do not use these techniques unless there is no other choice.

One signal to run away is when a tricky, or flashy move (suggesting experience) is performed by someone holding a knife. Keep in mind that sometimes a simple blocking kick to the attacker's knee may effectively ward off this kind of knife wielding attacker. Next, several proven techniques will be explored in detail to defend a knife attack.

## Using "Running Away" as a Trick

When attacked by a knife-wielding opponent (figure 27a), your first reaction should be to pretend to run away (figure 27b). Instead of truly running away, suddenly stop and sta-

Fig. 27a

Fig. 27b

Fig. 27c

Fig. 27d

Fig. 27e

bilize yourself to deliver an explosive back-kick to the attacker's leading knee with no hesitation (figure 27c). This will cause serious damage to the assailant's knee. Take advantage at this point and turn around to deliver a heavy sweeping kick to his lead leg in order to unbalance him (figures 27d, e). After the opponent falls to the ground, you can kick his head using another sweeping kick to completely destroy his fighting potential (not shown).

This is a very effective technique and seems very simple. However, it requires a lot of practice to really understand the timing and balance. The key point for this technique is to use the timing difference between your stop and the attacker's reactionary stop, so that you will have time to prepare for your explosive kick at his unprotected knee and he will not be able to escape from your trick. This technique is not only designed for knife defense, but also useful against a stronger attacker without weapons.

### Arm-Lock Technique Against a Knife Threat

When grabbed and threatened (but not actually physically assaulted) by a knife in the face, as shown in figure 28a, your initial reaction should be to lean back away from the knife, while raising one of your hands (using a leaning motion) and capturing the opponent's knife-holding hand by surprise (figure 28b). This coordinated whole body motion creates an opportunity to put the opponent in an arm-lock as shown in figure 28c.

Practitioners of this technique note that this leaning-back motion also enhances body rotation (by shortening the turning radius) and extending the opponent's grabbing arm (lever arm) in order to use leverage for the arm-lock. By speed and surprise, well-trained arm-lock techniques are excellent for dealing with knife threats that have not progressed to actual knife ("immediate") attacks.

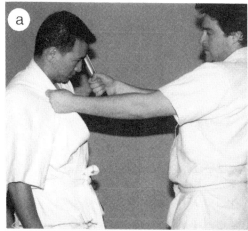

Fig. 28a

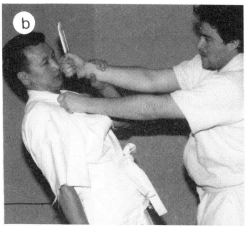

Fig. 28b

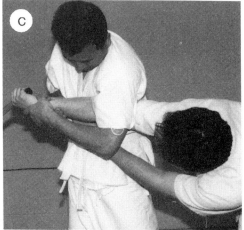

Fig. 28c

## Arm-Lock Techniques Against Immediate Knife Attacks

### Defense Against Over-Hand Knife Strikes:

When attacked by a powerful over-hand knife attack (a common method of knife attacking), quickly charge the attacker as soon as he is committed to his attack in order to intercept and block his arm with both hands as shown in figures 29a, b. This two-hand block (figure 29b) is designed to avoid injuring the thumb of the grappling hand, which is a common injury when trying to grab an over-hand knife strike with only one hand. The "charging" motion is further intended to catch the opponent's knife-holding hand as early as possible so that he will not be able to trick you by playing with the distance between you. Immediately after blocking, follow his force in a sudden motion and redirect his knife-holding hand to the other side, as shown in figure 29c, then lock and break his arm using your whole body weight and shake down on it (figure 29d).

Fig. 29a

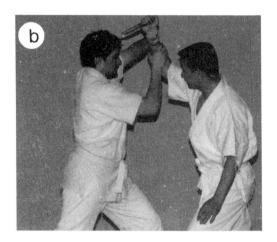

Fig. 29b

Fig. 29c

Fig. 29d

## Defense Against a Linear Knife Attack:

To prevail against a linear, stepping-in knife attack (figure 30a, b), the initial (solid) block is essential to ensure personal safety (figure 30b). Whether or not you can catch and lock the attacker's arm after the block is not as important as your safety! Catching his knife-holding hand and turning his knife back to him is the optimal choice in this matter, however.

In this technique, block his knife attack (at your chest or face) as shown in figure 30b, catch it, and redirect his knife back to him by using the natural bending of his arm with the help of your other hand (figure 30d). This technique only works well to deal with a stepping-in type of knife attack (linear form) in the body positions where the attacker holds his knife in his lead hand while your leading hand is on the same side as his knife holding hand as shown in figures 30a, b. In other words, this technique is dependent on body position.

Fig. 30a

Fig. 30b

Fig. 30c

Fig. 30d

To summarize this seminar, three important guiding principles are reiterated. These principles will assist readers in creating their own version of the techniques and to deal with changing situations. The principles are:

1) Safety is the primary priority when dealing with any form of knife attack. When possible, running away is the best policy.

2) Pretending to be scared can help hide an attempt for a surprise counter-attack.

3) It is extremely difficult to deal with a trained knife attacker who uses tricky moves. It is a signal to run away and forget about any attempt to subdue a knife-wielding assailant when you see an aggressor preparing his knife attack by feinting and faking.

# SEMINAR 6

## Surprise Techniques
## • A Military Approach •

SURPRISE TECHNIQUES - A MILITARY APPROACH • 71

What is a primary reason behind military successes? Often, it is based on the element of surprise that leads to dominating the opponent. Achieving the element of surprise often requires the development of information about the enemy—for example, where he'll be at a certain time and what resources he might have while at that location.

A classical method to obtain "surprise" information is to send military special forces behind enemy lines to capture enemy soldiers. Once beyond enemy lines, control techniques delivered to the blind side of an unsuspecting opponent are extremely useful. Examples of techniques that implement this strategy include the traditional "figure eight" tie (figure 31j) to conclusively render an opponent helpless, once dominated by a surprise attack from behind.

Of course, an opponent must first be subdued before a technique such as the figure eight tie can be employed. Subduing an opponent requires use of certain principles. These include:

1) It must be a surprising attack.

2) It must be one against one and without the need of any special equipment.

3) It is used to control an opponent by skill, but not to kill.

4) It must be equally effective when dealing with a stronger opponent.

5) It does not require long-term training to master.

To illustrate the use of these principles in performing surprise techniques, two skills will be reviewed in this seminar. These are favorite "enemy capture" skills of the Chinese Army. For civilians, these methods can be used to defend oneself or family against a violent person who is stronger and could not be controlled by ordinary, face-to-face methods.

## Knee-Hold from Behind

Soldier A has snuck up and managed to position himself behind Soldier B. Soldier A quickly steps in and holds Soldier B's knees with his front shoulder against Soldier B's bottom (figure 31a, b). By this method, Soldier B will not be able to escape from Soldier A's hold. Next, Soldier A will take Soldier B down by an explosive pulling power (figure 31c) by pulling hard and low against Soldier B's knees. Soldier B's unexpected fall may injure his face and hands, depending on the surface nature of the ground.

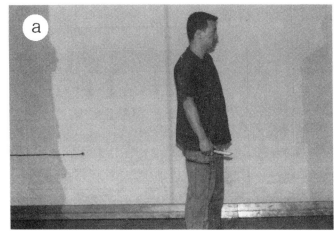

Fig. 31a

Fig. 31b

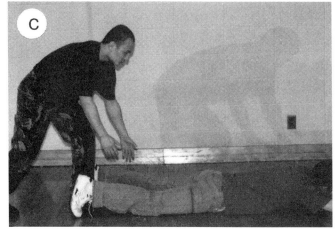

Fig. 31c

Now, Soldier A takes advantage of Soldier B's injury and position to ride on his back, striking the back of Soldier B's neck (a very sensitive and lethal target) with his right palm (figure 31d, e) and continuously applies pressure on it (figure 31f), so that Soldier B's face will be forced into the ground. This causes Soldier B to instinctively keep his face off the ground.

Soldier A takes advantage again to insert his left arm for a strangle hold as shown in figure 31g. Soldier A should keep this hold until Soldier B completely loses his fighting potential (not too long or too hard so as not to kill).

Fig. 31d

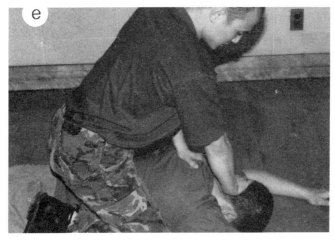

Fig. 31e

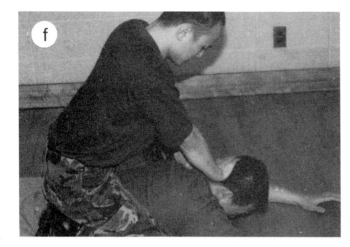

Fig. 31f

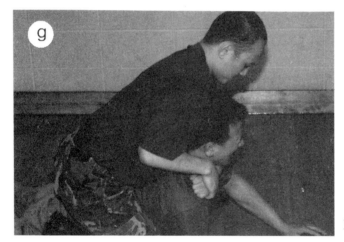

Fig. 31g

## Figure Eight Tie-Up

Now it is time to tie up and completely subdue Soldier B. Soldier A releases his strangle-hold and picks up Soldier B's two naturally falling arms (figure 31h). Next, he pulls them backward, while riding forward on Soldier B's upper back in order to trap his two arms on Soldier A's upper thighs (figure 31i). Thus, Soldier A can free at least one of his hands to tie Soldier B by using the figure eight tie-up method as shown in figure 31j.

The upper loop of the figure eight is localized around the neck, while the bottom loop is localized around Soldier B's arms. This figure eight tie-up is the best method to completely subdue an opponent. It is virtually impossible to escape from this technique. If a rope is not available, one can be easily made with green, wet grass in the immediate environment. Grass rope does have necessary strength as long as it is kept wet.

Soldier A's final move is to insert a towel into Soldier B's mouth so that he is unable to make any sound. Soldier B can then be carried away (figure 31k) and eventually interrogated for information.

The "enemy capture" skill described here is a very dangerous technique. It was not designed for civilian use. Aside from the military, it may also be useful for police officers to use to apprehend suspects. However, knowledge of this skill may be used in civilian situations to save a friend or a loved one from (anticipated) criminal aggression. For instance, by controlling a stronger attacker from behind who is threatening someone, you can create an opportunity to subdue the aggressor successfully.

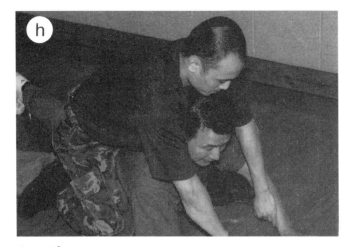

Fig. 31h

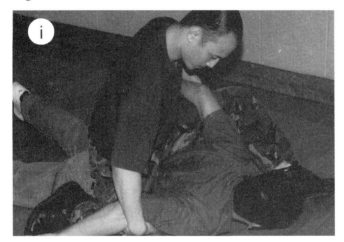

Fig. 31i

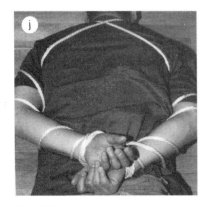

Fig. 31j

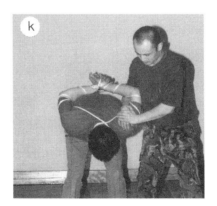

Fig. 31k

# APPENDIX

## A Case Analysis:
## Holyfield vs. Tyson

Although arguably considered the stronger fighter, professional boxer Mike Tyson has been upset twice by Evander Holyfield. Many comments have been published about these seemingly strange victories. Rather than anecdotal analysis of Holyfield's surprising victories, in this case analysis of the bouts will be assessed from a scientific point of view. This will equip readers with the principles that truly govern victory against seemingly insurmountable opponents.

It is commonly understood that striking power is of utmost importance in boxing. Striking power, as mentioned in seminar one, is the change in momentum (body weight, or force, times speed) divided by the time it took to change. In other words, a fast moving object with a certain weight is the "striking power" whenever it is decelerated or stopped.

This is why speed and body weight are important in punching power. Furthermore, effective strikes are characterized by the shortest time and distance required to initiate or generate a technique. Well-trained boxers have well-conditioned muscle force and know how to use it correctly. They require a relatively short time and distance to prepare their power strikes. However, as with any technique, these power strikes still require some minimal time and distance to deliver an effective strike.

Mike Tyson's power strike is characterized by his quick initiation combined with a well-coordinated whole-body motion. Mike initiates his strike with a strong "stepping force" on the ground (similar to that of a sprinter), and his whole body landing or "shaking" down just as he lands his punch. This takes advantage of his strong legs and more centralized body shape which can be coordinated easily. However, his kind of power strike depends on the success of his "short sprint," which also serves as a disadvantage. In fact, Holyfield consistently interrupted Tyson's "short sprint," shaking-down motion and thereby disabled the powerful punches of Tyson.

Under careful analysis, it is evident that Tyson was consistently hurt by the strong counter punches of Holyfield (who launched his counters at the instant Tyson committed to his attack). Not only did this neutralize Tyson, it also destroyed his "safe instinct." It is very difficult to overcome this instinctive fear, no matter how tough one may be. This explains why Tyson's striking speed and gap-closing speed were obviously reduced after the first round.

In both unarmed combat and self-defense, power strikes have to be initiated safely so that one does not worry about himself. Otherwise, the human instinct of fear will affect the speed of a power strike by initiating the strike with hesitation. Therefore, safely closing the gap between you and your opponent is fundamental to a powerful strike.

Mike Tyson has very advanced "closing in" skills which makes use of a technique called angulation. He usually goes down and sideways slightly (to avoid a counter) as he is closing the gap. This "relative safe angle" in closing usually allows him to initiate his strikes without hesitation or fear. Besides the advantage of safely closing the gap, this down and sideward motion also provides a power source for his slightly angular punch. Due to the joint structure of the human fist, a slightly angular strike (rather than a straight punch) provides optimal power because it generates less joint/muscle tendon friction during the motion.

In addition to generating or neutralizing power as just discussed, reach is also very important while analyzing Holyfield versus Tyson. A longer reach can potentially neutralize speed and power if used correctly. Holyfield's longer reach was put to good use by always countering Tyson's first strike. In effect, this destroyed the continuity of Tyson's combinations.

It appears that these distance and timing concerns are another important revelation of Holyfield's strategy against Tyson. The most important element in timing is to initiate a counter whenever the opponent is committed to his attack. In essence, one would want to catch the opponent on a rush so that he would not be able to escape the counter. This is especially effective when facing an opponent with fast hands and a long reach. It is also very clear that use of this technique requires safely closing the gap either by safe angles or by proper blocking.

Correct judgment on distance is also required. Holyfield counter-charged Tyson whenever he sensed Tyson was committed to his attack. Again, this neutralized Tyson's power since he was intercepted early before he reached his ideal distance where he is inarguably most dangerous.

Furthermore, Holyfield used his longer arms (with his elbows as a shield) to destroy Tyson's confidence and cause Tyson to instinctively fear coming in for an attack. Meanwhile, Holyfield was able to predict Mike's preparatory gestures and speed. The result was quite literally shooting Tyson down, just as one would shoot a flying duck by aiming just a little in front of it's path of flight. This caused Mike to directly charge into Evandor's low aiming counter-strikes and, as mentioned earlier, the full deceleration of a moving object generates maximum power. In other words, the meeting of two forces always causes more damage than a single force.

Observers will also note that Holyfield goes slightly sideways when counter-charging or attacking Tyson. This provided a safe angle to close-the-gap and made Tyson charge into one of Holyfield's elbows. Repeatedly, Holyfield's low aiming counter-strikes neutralized Tyson's charge and caught Tyson just as he tried to close-the-gap.

If Holyfield and Tyson engage in a rematch, Tyson could win if he develops a correct strategy to direct his training. Power, and especially speed, are critical for boxing success and will lead to victory if used correctly. Tyson should concentrate on counter-strikes and employ them whenever Holyfield is committed to his attacks!

Decisive strikes should focus on second or third strikes of a combination while the first move should be used for countering. The counter-charge itself may cause an opponent to be in an unfavorable position and set up a decisive strike (with the second strike). This strategy may require Tyson to force Holyfield to strike by trying to encroach upon his territory to the point where Holyfield feels threatened enough to deliver the first strike and commit himself. Only then should Mike use his quick head movement, speed, and power to safely close-the-gap to a distance where he is dangerous and deliver his own counter strikes.

In summary, the victory by Evandor Holyfield against Mike Tyson was a victory directed by correct fighting strategy and universal, scientific principles. Although many fans considered Tyson a sure winner due to his raw strength and fierce determination, Holyfield's victory illustrates what can be achieved by use of certain principles. Whether an opponent is larger, stronger, or faster, readers of *Effective Techniques for Unarmed Combat and Self-Defense* have the same opportunity for a "Goliath" victory as Holyfield by using the outlined principles presented in the various seminars of the text.

# References

Huang, Bin. (1996). *Shuaijiao: Chinese Style Wrestling*. Beijing, PRC: Ren Min Ti Chu Ban She (People's Publications).

Zhang, Xia & Huang, Bin. (1998). *Wrestling*. Beijing, PRC: Zhi Shi Chu Ban She (Knowledge Publications).